A Wandering Walk Guidebook:

St. Louis, MO - Downtown

Tom Alyea

ISBN-13: 978-1516973262

ISBN-10: 1516973267

CONTENTS

ACKNOWLEDGMENTS

Special thanks goes to the volunteers at the St. Louis Visitor Center and The National Park Service for all their help in identifying the fantastic places to walk in Independence.

1
WALKING TOUR MAP

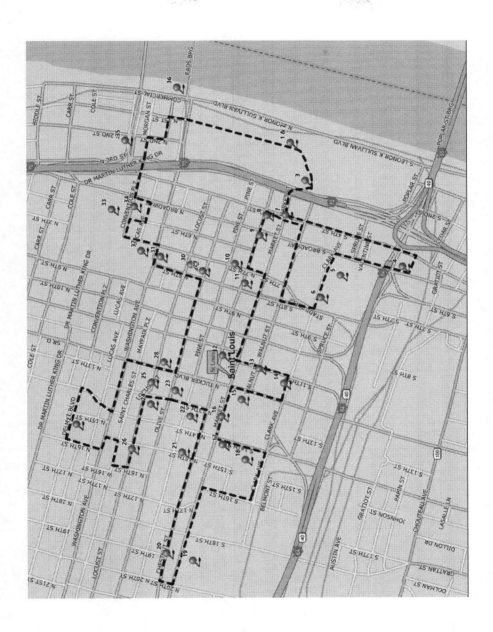

2
WALKING TOUR

Welcome to St. Louis, MO! You will begin your 8-mile walking tour directly beneath the most iconic landmark in St. Louis, and possibly in the entire United States – The Gateway Arch. The nation's tallest monument represents what the entire city of St. Louis is all about – a gateway to the West. The history of St. Louis is intimately tied to the epic era of migration and settlement of the West in the early 19th century. Even before that day in 1803 when Thomas Jefferson signed the Louisiana Purchase, St. Louis has been an important part of the westward migration and settlement of the country.

In 1764, Pierre Laclede held in his hands a land grant from the King of France. Laclede was a fur trader and needed to establish a fur trading post along the Mississippi River. With his 13-year-old scout, Auguste Chouteau, Laclede chose a parcel of land near the confluence of the Mississippi and Missouri Rivers. A year later, construction was completed on a small village and trading post. Laclede named the village St. Louis in honor of King Louis the IX of France. While most of the inhabitants of the village were French, that didn't last long. In 1770, as part of a treaty to end the Seven Years' War in Europe, France ceded control of its Louisiana Territory in North America to Spain. For the next 30 years, the Spanish crown owned the land where St. Louis was founded. In 1800, a secret treaty with Napoleon transferred the Louisiana Territory back to France. Once again, the city of St. Louis was under the French flag. Napoleon didn't control this area of North America for long. In the early 1800's, France was in desperate need of funds to maintain its armies while Napoleon tried to conquer much of Europe. In 1803, President Thomas Jefferson negotiated with France to purchase the Louisiana Territory. For approximately $15 million dollars the size of the United States nearly doubled. St. Louis was now under control of the Americans. Legend has it that on the day of transfer of the Louisiana Purchase, St. Louis flew under three flags – French, Spanish, and American.

To gain a greater understanding of exactly what he had just purchased, Thomas Jefferson needed a small group of men to explore the lands west of the Mississippi River. St. Louis grew in fame as the starting point for the expeditions of Meriwether Lewis and William Clark. When Lewis and Clark brought back news of the riches of the West, the small village of St. Louis exploded into a full size city. Thousands of fur trappers, traders, farmers, and business men flooded the town eager to find fame and fortune in the western frontier. In 1823, the population had grown to the point that the city could be incorporated.

For the next 50 years, the population of St. Louis continued to grow. The city became the most important center of commerce on the Mississippi River. During this time, the predominately French population of the city was overrun with immigrants from other parts of Europe. A revolution in Germany caused many of that country's population to move to the United States. As the German immigrants moved west, they saw that the landscape around St. Louis looked like their German homeland. During the 1850's, a beer brewer named George Schneider sold his struggling business to an up-and coming business man named Eberhard Anheuser. Adolphus Busch, who was the first American brewer to use pasteurization to keep beer fresh, joined forces with Eberhard Anheuser to form the Anheuser-Busch Brewing Company. The efforts of these two immigrants seeking a better life in the U.S. are seen today with every bottle of Budweiser sold. At this same time, the Irish Potato Famine saw thousands of Irish immigrants move into the city of St. Louis. Italian, Serbian, Syrian, and Greek immigrants also helped to build the rich culture that is St. Louis today.

St. Louis became a strategic location during the American Civil War. St. Louis, at the start of the Civil War in 1861, already had a strong Union Army presence. Throughout the war, the city was firmly in the control of the Union Army. No major battles were ever fought in or near the city. Another factor that added to this was the loyal German population of the city. The Germans were opposed to slavery and firmly in support of maintaining a strong, united nation.

After the Civil War, the population of St. Louis continued its rapid growth. In 1876, voters approved a separation from St. Louis County. The city became the first in the nation to establish a 'home rule' charter. To this day, the city operates under its own charter, separate from the much larger county of St. Louis. By 1900, the city was the largest manufacturing center in the region. Because of access to rail and water transportation, the city became one of the largest commerce areas in the nation. The 1874 construction of the Eads Bridge linked St. Louis to the eastern areas of the United States. This allowed even more manufactured goods and agricultural products to move in to and out of the city.

1904 was perhaps the greatest year in the city of St. Louis. In 1904, the city was host to both a World's Fair and the Olympic Games. During the

1904 Louisiana Purchase Exposition World's Fair, more than 20 million people traveled to St. Louis to witness this great spectacle. For nearly a year, the most popular song in America was "Meet me in St. Louis, Louis." Many of the buildings constructed for the Fair were temporary. But, there are some remaining, and important, structures still existing today. Most of these are in the Forest Park area of St. Louis. Forest Park was the site of the Exposition and is located about five miles west of downtown. As part of the World's Fair Exposition, St. Louis also hosted the 1904 Summer Olympic Games. These were the first Olympic games held in the United States. 12 nations were represented at these games. Unfortunately, with rising political tensions in Europe and the Russo-Japanese War in progress, the number of athletes from around the world who participated was limited. One of the most remarkable athletes was an American gymnast, George Eyser, who won six medals even though his left leg was made of wood.

As the 19th century progressed, St. Louis continued to prosper and grow. Second only to the Detroit area, the city was the largest automobile production center in the nation. Many people think the traffic in St. Louis is bad today, and that may be so, because downtown St. Louis was seeing traffic jams as early as 1925. The city is the home to the first automobile accident in the nation. During World War I and World War II, the city's manufacturing facilities were turning out tanks, guns, and other supplies at rates not seen in other parts of the nation. At the end of World War II, the city had reached a point where growth could only move outwards and into the suburbs of St. Louis County. This created a huge shift for St. Louis as, for the first time in its history, the population began to decline. This population decline saw the city fall into disrepair, ruin, and increased crime.

By the 1960's, the construction of the Gateway Arch, Busch Memorial Stadium (home of the Cardinals Baseball team), and other major building projects led to a revitalization of the downtown St. Louis area you will see today. This revitalization continues to this day with a restoration of Union Station and other buildings throughout the downtown area. Along with Busch Stadium, you will be walking by the Scott Trade Center, home of the St. Louis Blues hockey team, and the Edward Jones Dome, where the St. Louis Rams football team plays.

It's time to tighten those shoelaces, grab your water bottle and begin...

> ➤ **Start your walking tour by standing directly beneath the Gateway Arch.**

Stop 1:
The Gateway Arch
(Market St.)

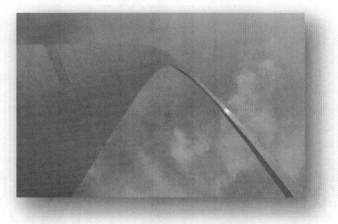

As you stand at the base of the Gateway Arch, look upwards to the top 630-feet above you. You are seeing the tallest national monument in the United States, the tallest building in the state of Missouri, and the largest stainless steel structure in the world. The Arch was built as a monument to honor the Westward expansion of the United States. It is the centerpiece of the National Park Services Jefferson National Expansion Memorial.

The history of the Gateway Arch goes back to the early 1930's. Civic Leader, Luther Smith, came up with an idea to revitalize the St. Louis riverfront area. As this was during the time of the Great Depression, the idea to generate jobs and stimulate the economy was also important. Smith envisioned a national memorial to the westward expansion of America. In 1933, a St. Louis City Council meeting was held and the city approved the formation of Jefferson National Expansion Memorial Association (JNEMA). In December 1933, President Franklin D. Roosevelt signed an Executive Order approving the memorial as the first National Historic Site in the nation. Due to limited funds and the onset of World War II, little activity occurred on the memorial for most of the 1930's and early 1940's.

As the war was winding down, Luther Smith began a big drive to complete the memorial. In 1944, Smith met with the Director of the National Park Service, Newton Drury, to discuss the design of the memorial. He proposed that the memorial should be a design that was "transcending in spiritual and aesthetic values." Smith always felt that the design of the memorial should contain one central feature, "a single shaft, a building, an arch, or something else that would symbolize American culture and civilization."

In 1945, JNEMA was officially inaugurated and their first piece of business was to announce that an architectural contest would be held to determine the design of the memorial. The design competition would be in two-stages. The first stage would be an open competition for any architect around the world to design the memorial. The second stage would narrow down the competition to a small handful of designs that would be judged based on their proposals. By 1947, the first stage of competition was completed and the 172 submissions were narrowed down by a jury organized by JNEMA to 5 designs.

One of those designs was by Finish American architect Eero Saarinen. In his proposal, Saarinen wrote:

> *The arch symbolized the gateway to the West, the national expansion, and whatnot.*

After much deliberation, and several delays, in 1948 the jury chose Saarinen's design on a unanimous vote. Several months later, the National Park Service also approved the design.

It took over a decade to purchase the land, clear away old buildings, and re-route railroad tracks. Finally, in 1959, ground was broken on the memorial. In 1961, the foundation of the structure was laid. It wasn't until 1962 that the first piece of stainless steel was put into place. The stainless steel triangles, which narrow as they move to the top of the arch, were raised by specially designed cranes and derricks.

On October 28, 1965, the final piece of the arch, the keystone at the very top, was set into place. Vice President Hubert Humphrey watched the topping out ceremony from a helicopter hovering nearby. As a Catholic Priest and a rabbi prayed, a short, 10-ton piece of stainless steel triangle was lowered onto the top of the arch. But, there was a small problem. The 8-foot long section wasn't going to fit. Due to various delays, the topping out ceremony was held later than planned and the heat of the sun had constricted the two sides of the arch and the final piece was five inches too long. For a while, there were worries if the two sides of the arch would ever

8

meet in the middle. Using firehouses to cool the sides of the arch, and hydraulic jacks to pry apart the sides, the final piece was lowered and welded into place.

While the topping out ceremony was completed in 1965, it would be another two years before the Gateway Arch was opened to the public. The original visitors center and tram began operation on July 24, 1967. The arch was officially dedicated by Hubert Humphrey on May 25, 1968. In his statements Humphrey said:

> *"The arch is a soaring curve in the sky that links the rich heritage of yesterday with the richer future of tomorrow."*

As the Arch celebrates its 50th Anniversary, millions of visitors from around the world come to view this marvel of engineering and reflect on the Westward expansion of the United states. And most will take the short tram ride up to the top of the arch. The deck at the top of the arch is 65 feet long and about 7 feet across. Small windows offer views up to 30 miles away. On windy days, you can feel the arch sway below you as you gaze out westward towards the city of St. Louis and beyond.

> ➤ **Walk inside the Visitor Center at the base of the Arch.**

Stop 2:
Museum of Westward Expansion
(Below the Arch)

Underneath the arch is the visitors center and the Museum of Westward Expansion. As you walk into the visitor centers, you are greeted by a full-length bronze statue of President Thomas Jefferson. Looking at the statue you see, in Jefferson's casual pose, how seamlessly he was able to move among his many interests. He was a farmer, an architect, a statesman, an ambassador, and the 3rd President of the United States. His signing of the Louisiana Purchase allowed the United States to double its size and move the nation Westward across the Mississippi River to the Pacific Ocean.

The Museum of Westward Expansion honors Jefferson and those pioneers who sought a better life in America. Inside the museum are exhibits that explore the early days of St. Louis and the role the city played in the migration that took place in the early 19th century. You can learn about the travels of Lewis and Clark, the trappers and mountain men, and other explorers.

The museum is also the starting point for the tram ride to the top of the arch. Prior to traveling up 630 feet to the top, an award-winning film will give you background on the Westward expansion of the U.S. and history of the Gateway Arch.

> ➤ **Exit the Visitor Center and follow the sidewalk and signs south to Stop 3 – The Old Cathedral.**

Stop 3:
The Old Cathedral
(209 Walnut Street)

The Basilica of Saint Louis, King of France was formerly called the Cathedral of Saint Louis. Today, it is referred to as the Old Cathedral. It was the first cathedral west of the Mississippi River. The Cathedral is named for King Louis IX of France, the same king the city of St. Louis is named after. There are two Catholic basilicas in St. Louis. The other, far larger, basilica is located about 5 miles to the west.

The earliest church structure on this site was built by the founder of the city, Pierre Laclede. A log cabin structure was used until 1818 when a brick church was constructed. The building you see before you today was constructed in 1834 and exists as a parish church to this day. Hundreds of buildings around the Jefferson National Memorial and Gateway Arch were cleared away to make room for the National Park that was created in the mid-20th century. This church is one of the few remaining buildings that did not get razed.

In 1961, Pope John XXIII designated this church as a basilica to honor its long history. John XXIII named the cathedral the Basilica of Saint Louis, King of France.

As you face the Bascilica, you will see two engravings in gold. The first engraving has the words "In honorem s. Ludovici. Deo uni et trino dicatum. A. MDCCCXXXIV" carved in the stone. This Latin is translated as "In honor of St. Louis. Dedicated to the one and triune God. A.D. 1834." The larger gold engraving is the word "Yahweh" you see over the main entrance of the cathedral. But, pity the poor engraver since he made a typo. The Hebrew letters actually translate to "Yachuch."

Many artifacts from the church are stored in the basement. These artifacts tell the history of the Roman Catholic Archdiocese of St. Louis. In the basement is a bell that was given to the church by the French governor of the Louisiana Territory in the early 1800's. The body of Bishop Joseph Rosati is interred in a vault under the sanctuary. Rosati was the bishop who ordered the construction of the current church you see today.

> ➢ **Facing the front of the Cathedral, turn left on Walnut St. and cross over pedestrian bridge.**
> ➢ **Continue on Market St. to 4th St.**
> ➢ **Left on 4th St.**
> ➢ **Right on Cerre St. to Stop 4.**

Stop 4:
Eugene Field House and Toy Museum
(634 S. Broadway)

The Eugene Field House and St. Louis Toy Museum was the home of the man who is best known as the "Children's Poet." Born in 1850, Eugene Field is most famous for the poem *"Wynken, Blynken, and Nod."* Although Fields was a journalist by trade, he began writing light-hearted children's poems early in his career. His first published book of poetry was written in 1879. This book, called *Christmas Treasures*, appeared in an anthology called *A Little Book of Western Verse.* Fields published over a dozen volumes of children's poetry books before his death in 1895.

Eugene Fields' father, Roswell, was a renowned attorney. Roswell was the attorney who filed a lawsuit on behalf of Dred and Harriet Scott. The Scott's were two slaves seeking their freedom. The case eventually went to the Supreme Court of the United States and was a major issue that helped hasten the start of the American Civil War.

> ➤ **Cross S. Broadway St. and turn right.**
> ➤ **Continue to Broadway St. to Stop 5.**

Stop 5:
Busch Stadium
(700 Clark St.)

As you walk up Broadway, you can't miss Busch Stadium on your left. Busch Stadium is the home of the St. Louis Cardinals, St. Louis' Major League Baseball team. Around town, the stadium is referred to as the "New Busch Stadium" or "Busch Stadium III." This stadium was completed in 2006.

The current Busch Stadium replaced Busch Memorial Stadium (also known as Busch Stadium II). A portion of that stadium's former footprint is found in the new stadium. The remainder of the old stadium property was turned into a commercial area called Ballpark Village, which you will pass by on your way to the next stop.

The first St. Louis Cardinal's stadium was called Sportsman's Park, which was renamed Busch Stadium in 1953. From 1966-2006, the St. Louis Cardinals played in Busch Stadium II.

The Cardinals are one of the oldest teams in major league baseball. They can date their first games back to 1881. The Cardinals have won 11 World Series Championships.

> ➢ **Turn left on Clark Ave.**
> ➢ **Continue on Clark Ave to Stop 6.**

Stop 6:
Cardinal's Hall of Fame Statues
(700 Clark St.)

The St. Louis Cardinals major league baseball team has been around for over 110 years. Throughout that time, the team has seen some of the greatest players of their day pitch, hit, and run the bases. These players were an important part of St. Louis winning 19 National League pennants and 11 World Series Championships.

At the main entrance to Busch Stadium, some of the greatest ball players for the St. Louis Cardinals are honored with statues of their likeness. These include:

Stan Musial – Musial is considered to be one of the greatest hitters in baseball history with 17 Major League Baseball and 29 National League records.

Dizzy Dean – Dean was the last National League pitcher to win 30 games in one season.

Ozzie Smith – Nicknamed "The Wizard," Smith was an outstanding defensive player, 13-consecutive year winner of the Golden Glove, and played in 15 All-Star games.

> ➢ **Right on 8th St.**
> ➢ **Right on Walnut St.**
> ➢ **Left on 4th St. to Stop 7.**

Stop 7:
International Fur Exchange Building
(214 S. 4th St.)

Fur trading started in St. Louis as early as 1764. This 7-story building is a final link to the history of fur trading in the city. In the early 1900's, St. Louis was a major fur trading center in the nation. After many years of record growth, the fur traders came to the conclusion they needed a new location for their business. They built this large warehouse in 1919 to display and auction fur pelts. Traders were impressed with the lighting design of the building, which provided outstanding ways to showcase fur pelts headed to auction. All the way through the 1940's, eighty percent of the world's seal, beaver, fox, and other pelts were auctioned in this building.

By the 1950's, the fur trading business began a steep decline as the public began to purchase fewer fur coats and other products made from fur. The final fur auction was held in this building in 1956. For over 40 years, the building sat abandoned until the owners of the Drury Hotel chain purchased the building and renovated it into a hotel.

> ➢ **Continue on 4ᵗʰ St. to Stop 8.**

Stop 8:
The Old Courthouse
(11 N. 4ᵗʰ St.)

The Old St. Louis County Courthouse was built as both a federal and state courthouse. Originally built in 1839, the courthouse was extensively remodeled in 1864 with the addition of the large dome and two large building wings. Architect William Rumbold designed the cast iron dome based on St. Peter's Basilica in Vatican City. The dome also resembles the dome of the U.S. Capitol building in Washington, D.C. Both domes were built at approximately the same time. The dome has four lunettes with paintings by Carl Wimar. These large paintings depict four major events in the history of St. Louis. For thirty years, from 1864 to 1894, the Old Courthouse was the tallest building in the state of Missouri. The building is no longer used as a courthouse and is operated by the National Park Service as part of the Jefferson National Expansion Memorial.

Several landmark court cases that eventually went to the U.S. Supreme Court started in this courthouse. In 1872, Virginia Minor walked to her local polling location to vote. This was before women had the right to vote in the United States. Minor, a women's suffrage activist, was denied the right to vote and sued the county election board. Her trials, including testimony before the Missouri Supreme Court, were held in this building. Eventually the case made it to the U.S. Supreme Court. She lost. The Supreme Court upheld the male-only voting rules. The court stressed that, at that time, the Constitution did not address voting rules. Those rules were handled by the individual states.

The most famous court case to be held in the Old Courthouse was in 1846. A slave by the name of Dred Scott, sued for his and his wife's freedom. It was thought that Scott stood on solid legal ground. Since the early 1800's, Missouri had a legal precedent that stated that slaves freed because of their prolonged residence in a free state would remain free when returned back to Missouri, a slave state. As Scott had lived with his slaveholder in free state Illinois for a number of years, it was assumed that Scott and his wife were free persons when they were forced to move back to Missouri.

The case was ultimately decided by the U.S. Supreme Court in 1857. The case, Dred Scott v. Sandford, ruled against the Scotts. The court basically said that the Scotts, as slaves, were not citizens of the U.S. and therefore could not sue. Chief Justice Roger N. Taney believed that this settled the question of slavery once and for all. But, he was wrong. It had the opposite effect and was one of the reasons for the start of the American Civil War in 1861.

The Old Courthouse saw its last case in 1930. The building was soon abandoned as new Federal and State courthouses were built in St. Louis. As part of President Franklin Roosevelts executive order to declare the area around the Old Courthouse, and the site of the future Gateway Arch, a national monument, the building was sold to the National Park Service. Today, visitors can view the renovated dome and the beautiful paintings inside the cupola. Two courtrooms have been restored to the days of the early trials. Periodically, the National Park Service will conduct mock trials, including the Dred Scott trial, with visitors from the audience playing key roles in the reenactment. Exhibits from the early days of the courthouse, St. Louis history, the Dred Scott Trials, and other historical items can be viewed inside.

> ➢ **Left on Chestnut.**
> ➢ **Continue on Chestnut walking to Olympic Running Statue in Stop 9.**

Stop 9:
Kiener Plaza
(Market and Chestnut Streets)

As you walk along Chestnut St., the open, park-like setting to your left is called Kiener Plaza. This 2 acre park was dedicated in 1962 as a memorial to Harry J. Kiener. Kiener was an amateur boxer, wrestler, and swimmer who was born in St. Louis in 1881. He is most famous for several medals he won in the 1904 St. Louis Olympics. Kiener was the captain of the U.S. Men's Track and Field team during those games.

The centerpiece of the plaza is a pool and fountain with a statue known as "The Runner." The statue was sculpted by William Zorach. Harry Kiener donated all the money needed to build the park, fountain, and statue.

> ➤ **Continue on Chestnut St. to 7ᵗʰ St.**
> ➤ **Look across 7ᵗʰ St. to your right for Stop 10.**

Stop 10:
Wainwright Building
(709 Chestnut St.)

The red-brick Wainwright Building is perhaps one of the most famous skyscrapers in the world. It is listed as one of "10 Buildings That Changed America" in a recent Architectural Digest Magazine poll. It was the first skyscraper that really looked like one. The building was designed by noted architect, Louis Sullivan, who is considered to be the "Father of Skyscrapers." The 10-story red brick office building was completed in 1891.

While other tall buildings were constructed previous to the Wainwright Building, this is the first building that used straight lines, even though heavily ornamented, as part of its design. Previous skyscrapers looked more like wedding cakes – several floors that were wider at the bottom and narrowed towards the top of the building. Using revolutionary design and construction techniques, Sullivan built a new kind of skyscraper. One that was beautiful and functional, but also one that rose at the same width from the ground floor to the top.

> ➤ **Cross 7th St. and turn Left on 7th St.**
> ➤ **Right on Market St. to Stop 11.**

Stop 11:
Gateway Mall and Citygarden
(Between Market and Chestnut Streets)

You are experiencing St. Louis's Citygarden as you walk the next two blocks along Market Street. Until 2009, this area, once known as the Gateway Mall, was little more than two empty blocks of grass. In July 2009, the three-acre Citygarden was dedicated as a space for outdoor sculptures, water features, and beautiful trees and flowers.

Public art is not new to downtown St. Louis. As early as the 1940s, a large work of art by the sculptor, Carl Milles, was installed outside Union Station. Another famous sculpture of eight large plates of weathering steel by Richard Serra was placed at the far west end of what is now Citygarden in 1962.

This urban oasis has meandering walkways that take you by large works of art resting on open lawns. 24 sculptures of both contemporary and modern design are placed throughout the park. There are no "Do Not Touch" signs in this park. Visitors are allowed to touch, walk around, even climb inside the sculptures. The six waterfalls, rain gardens, and the 102' Spray Plaza fountain offer soothing sounds in the busy downtown area.

Here are some of the more famous sculptures you will see as you wander through Citygarden:

- o "*Eros Bound*" by Igor Mitorai. This is a large bronze head laying sidewise on a granite circle. The granite is covered by a steady stream of flowing water. The sculpture is large enough to walk inside – and you are welcome to do so!
- o The large statue of Pinocchio is titled *Big White Gloves, Big Four Wheels*. Jim Dine sculpted this fun statue in 2009.
- o At Tenth Street you will find a large LED panel that displays two people walking. This work of art is called *Bruce and Sarah Walking* and was created by Julian Opie.
- o Towards the western end of Citygarden, you will see two bronze cast rabbits painted white. Although this work of art by Tom Claassen is untitled, locals refer to these as the *Two Rabbits*.

> ➢ **Continue on Market St. and through the Citygarden until you reach 11th St.**
> ➢ **Pause here at Market and 11th St. and look across 11th St. for Stop 12.**

Stop 12:
Civil Courts Building
(10 North Tucker Blvd.)

In 1923, the residents of St. Louis voted on a city bond that provided over $87 million for massive city improvements and the construction of a new Civil Courts Building to replace the Old Courthouse. The building you see today was completed in 1930.

The top of the 255' building was designed to resemble the tomb of Mausolus at Halicarnassus. This was considered to be one of the Seven Wonders of the Ancient World. It is also the origin of the word mausoleum.

The pyramidal-shaped roof of the building is made of cast aluminum. At the top of the building are two Greek sphinx-like figures. The figures have the bodies of a lion and the wings of an eagle. The fleur-de-lis of St. Louis are engraved on their chests.

The 22nd Judicial Circuit Court of Missouri continues to operate in this building.

> ➢ **Cross 11ᵗʰ St. and turn Left on 11ᵗʰ Street.**
> ➢ **Continue on 11ᵗʰ St. to Stop 13.**

Stop 13:
Winkelmeyer Building
(101 S. 11ᵗʰ St.)

This ornate building was originally constructed in 1903 as warehouse space for a printing company. For over 80 years it served as both a warehouse and office space for several companies. During the 1980's the building was abandoned and nearly razed. In late 1980, the Winkelmeyer Building was renovated as part of a major effort in downtown St. Louis to save historic structures and revitalize the area.

> ➤ **Continue on 11ᵗʰ St.**
> ➤ **Turn Right on Clark Ave. to Stop 14.**

Stop 14:
Municipal Services Building
(1100 Clark Ave.)

As part of the large 1923 city bond issue voted on by the residents of St. Louis City, many large structures were built in the downtown area. To maintain and provide power to the buildings, such as the Civil Courts Building and Kiel Opera House, a new Municipal Services Building was constructed in 1928.

This building once held a fire training academy, vehicle maintenance garage, and a large powerhouse that provided steam heating to twelve buildings in the area. In 1968, the powerhouse was shut down because the coal-fired boilers did not meet federal clean air requirements.

Portions of the old powerhouse structure were renovated into unique office spaces for small businesses. The garage portion of the building still is in operation as a public parking garage.

> ➤ **Continue on Clark St.**
> ➤ **Turn Right on Tucker Blvd.**
> ➤ **Turn Left on Market St. to Stop 15.**

Stop 15:
City Hall
(1200 Market St.)

This unique, and very large, structure is the St. Louis City Hall. The building was constructed between 1890 and 1904. The building continues to serve as City Hall.

The first thing you will notice is that the building used several types of materials during its construction. The reason for this is that the residents of the city would not pass bond issues to pay for the building. City Hall had to be built in stages when excess money was found in the city budget. The exterior of the first story is constructed of Missouri pink granite. The upper stories are made of orange Roman brick. Sandstone is used around the window openings.

Statues of the founder of St. Louis, Pierre Laclede, and General Ulysses S. Grant are located on the grounds of the building. The statue of Grant was originally located at the south entrance of City Hall where he stood next to a cannon. Residents were outraged that Grant's statue was placed at what was considered the back door of City Hall. His statue soon moved to the more prominent location you see today.

➤ **Continue on Market St. to Stop 16.**

Stop 16:
Municipal Courts Building
(1300 Market St.)

The Municipal Courts building is a three-story Bedford stone structure that was completed in 1911. For over 90 years, this was the site where the municipal courts for the city of St. Louis were located. Many city government offices were also located in the building. At the rear of the building was the city jail and juvenile courts.

In 2000, the Thomas Eagleton Federal Courthouse was completed and the municipal courts were moved to that building and other courthouse complexes in the downtown area. Today, the building is vacant. No decision has been made as to if the building will be razed or renovated.

> ➢ **Continue on Market St.**
> ➢ **Cross 14ᵗʰ St. and turn Left.**
> ➢ **Continue on 14ᵗʰ St. to Stop 17.**

Stop 17:
Kiel Auditorium
(Peabody Opera House)
(1300 Market St.)

Between 1934 and 1936 a state of the art Opera House and connected Municipal Convention Hall Auditorium were constructed in downtown St. Louis. The buildings were renamed the Kiel Auditorium upon the passing of popular St. Louis Mayor Henry Kiel in 1945. Today, the original structure has been greatly reduced in size. The 3,500-seat main theater of the Opera house is all that remains. The convention hall was demolished to build the Scottrade Auditorium in 1994. The Opera house is now called the Peabody Opera House.

Throughout the years, the Opera House has seen many entertaining and historic events. The first performance was in 1934 with a production of *Aida*. In that same year, the St. Louis Symphony Orchestra became the primary tenant of the building and would perform there until the 1960's. The St. Louis Symphony is the second oldest in the U.S.

One of the most historic political events of the 1948 presidential election occurred inside the auditorium. In 1948, President Harry S. Truman broadcast a speech on the last of his whistle-stop campaign tours as he campaigned to win re-election as President of the United States.

In 1965, a benefit concert with musical legends Frank Sinatra, Dean Martin, and Sammy Davis, Jr. was held in the Opera House. The concert was organized to raise money for a national halfway home for convicts. The overflow audience filled dozens of nearby halls where the concert could be viewed on closed-circuit television. It was the only time in the history of the Rat Pack's famous Vegas-style shows that was ever televised. The master of ceremony for the event was talk-show host Johnny Carson. The music was performed by the Count Basie Orchestra with Quincy Jones leading the band into some of the most famous musical numbers of the day.

Opera and theater shows were not the only events that took place in this ornate theater. Rock shows began performances in the 1970's. The most historic of all the rock concerts was held in 1978 when the Rolling Stones played in the sold-out theater. All 3,500 seats were sold out in 75-minutes after the show was announced.

The final performance in the Opera House occurred on May 4 1991. The St. Louis Philharmonic returned to the concert hall to close the theater down. The building remained closed until June 2010 when the Peabody Energy Company, along with community leaders, financed the renovation and re-opening of the Opera House. Aretha Franklin headlined the first performance at the new Peabody Opera House on October 1, 2011.

> ➤ **Continue on 14th St.**
> ➤ **Turn Right on Clark St. to Stop 18.**

Stop 18:
Scotttrade Center
(1401 Clark Ave.)

In 1992, the old Kiel Auditorium was torn down to make way for the new Kiel Center. This multipurpose arena opened in 1994. It is the home of the St. Louis Blues National Hockey League team. In 2006, naming rights for the building were sold to a St. Louis-based online brokerage firm. Today the building is called the Scottrade Center. Besides hockey, the arena is host to a wide range of events including concerts, professional wrestling, ice shows, and exhibitions.

As you walk in front of the arena you will see statues of famous St. Louis Blues hockey league All-Stars. These include:

- o   Brett Hull - Hull competed for Team USA in the 1998 and 2002 Winter Olympics, and played in the NHL for the St. Louis Blues from 1987 to 1998.
- o   Al MacInnis - MacInnis played in the NHL for the St. Louis Blues from 1976 to 1989.
- o   Bernie Federko - Federko played in the NHL for the St. Louis Blues from 1994 to 2004.

> ➤ **Continue on Clark St.**
> ➤ **Right on 16th St.**
> ➤ **Left on Market St. to Stop 19.**

Stop 19:
St. Louis Union Station
(1820 Market St.)

In 1894, St. Louis Union Station was completed at a cost of $6.5 million. Designer Theodore Link incorporated an eclectic mix of styles within the building, most notably a unique Romanesque style. The main concourse is nearly two blocks in length and once featured a luxurious hotel, a large dining hall, a saloon, ticket offices, gender-specific lounges, and office space. The ceiling of the Grand Hall was the world's first barrel-vaulted train concourse.

Today, the Grand Hall serves as a hotel registration area. But, when you wander inside you can see the majesty of what was once the world's largest and busiest train station. The Grand Hall is lighted by stained glass windows that depict the meeting of the East and West train routes. The most impressive stained-glass window is the "Allegorical Window" over the front entrance of the hall. This hand-made window was made entirely of Tiffany glass. The window features three women who represent the largest train stations of the 1890's: New York, St. Louis, and San Francisco.

Behind the Grand hall is the old train shed. Today, the train shed is a commercial and retail area for residents and visitors. The 11-acre train shed, made of giant sweeping arches, was once the largest single-span train shed in the world. It measured over 700' long and allowed forty-two trains to terminate so that passengers could enter and exit the trains in comfort. During the height of train service in the United States, St. Louis Union Station was home to 19 railroad companies and over 250 trains departed a day from the station. In anticipation of millions of visitors to the 1904 World's Fair, Union Station was expanded to accommodate all the passengers coming to town.

During the 1940's, Union Station was handling over 100,000 passengers a day. One of those passengers provided one of the most iconic photographs in history. In November 1948, Harry S. Truman had just learned that he won a close election for President of the United States. Truman had boarded a train in Independence, MO and was headed back to Washington D.C. During a stop in St. Louis, Truman picked up a newspaper with a headline that blazed "Dewey Defeats Truman." Truman walked to the end of his railcar and held up the newspaper for reporters to see.

During the 1950's and 1960's, railroad passenger service declined in the United States. Airlines became the preferred mode of long-distance travel. The massive Union Station became obsolete, and by the 1970's only 3 trains a day were leaving the station. By the 1980's, the remaining Amtrak passenger trains were moved to a smaller, more cost-efficient terminal about ½-mile away. Today, Union Station has been renovated to include shopping, dining, and hotel accommodations. The glory days of the railroads and Union Station can still be seen inside.

> ➢ **After walking around inside Union Station, return back to the front entrance on Market St.**
> ➢ **Left on Market St.**
> ➢ **Right on 20th St.**
> ➢ **Right on Chestnut St. to Stop 20.**

Stop 20:
Aloe Plaza
(Chestnut and Market Streets)

The 1923 bond issue that provided money for the Municipal Courts Building, Kiel Auditorium, and other large buildings in downtown St. Louis also allowed for the construction of greenways and plazas to help beautify the area.

.   Louis P. Aloe was the President of the Board of Alderman and was the leading proponent of the $87 million bond issue. When Mr. Aloe died in 1929, the plaza in front of Union Station was named in his honor.

The most impressive sculpture in the downtown area rests in Aloe Plaza. The sculpture and fountain, designed by Carl Milles, was completed in 1939. The statue is called *"Meeting of the Waters."*

> ➤ **Continue on Chestnut St. to Stop 21.**

Stop 21:
St. John the Apostle and Evangelist Catholic Church
(15 Plaza Square)

St. John the Apostle and Evangelist Parish was founded in 1847. It served Catholics moving to the first suburb of the original city of St. Louis. It's hard to imagine, but the area you see around you was once a peach orchard.

This church building was constructed in 1860 and has been in continuous use ever since. At one point in its history, the church was affiliated with the Archbasilica of St. John Lateran in Rome. This allowed the church to be referred to as a "Pope's Cathedral" and a Papal Canopy was once installed over the alter. The Papal Canopy meant that this church could conduct ordination and consecration services for new priests.

In 1864, James M. Slevin donated a large sculpture of The Madonna that was placed on the front of the alter. Slevin made this donation after his wife, Elizabeth, was tragically killed in an accident just months after they were married in the church. The face of The Madonna has the likeness of the young bride.

> ➤ **Continue on Chestnut St. to Stop 22.**

Stop 22:
Soldiers' Memorial
(1315 Chestnut St.)

In 1923, the residents of St. Louis voted to spend $6 million for a war memorial to honor those St. Louisans who lost their lives in World War I. Nearly all the money approved was spent on purchasing the land and little money was left to construct a building. It took another decade, and funds from the federal Relief and Recovery Act used during the Great Depression, to construct the Soldiers' Memorial. President Franklin D. Roosevelt dedicated the building in 1936.

Soldiers' Memorial is now a tribute to all the men and women who lost their lives in the wars this country has fought. To honor the service of those in the military, four huge sculptures were erected. These sculptures represent the virtues in a soldiers life: Courage, Vision, Loyalty, and Sacrifice.

The ceiling inside the memorial is made of mosaic tiles that form a large gold star. This ceiling is dedicated to the mothers of all the St. Louisans who have died in war.

> ➢ **Continue on Chestnut to 13ᵗʰ St.**
> ➢ **Left on 13ᵗʰ St. to Stop 23.**

Stop 23:
Missouri Pacific Building
(210 N. 13ᵗʰ St.)

This Art Deco style office building was built as the headquarters for the Missouri Pacific Railroad. The original plans called for the building to rise 35 stories into the sky, making it the tallest building in the city at the time. Construction began in 1928. However, the Great Depression impacted the work on the building. Rather than stop work, the owners of the building decided to end construction and the building only rose to 23 floors. In 1929, the Missouri Pacific Railroad began operations from this building.

The Missouri Pacific Railroad is one of the oldest in the state of Missouri. The railroad was the first to lay track west of the Mississippi River. MoPac goes back as far as 1849 when the original name of the railroad was the St. Louis Iron Mountain Railroad. By the 1870's, the railroad had operations all the way to the Pacific Ocean. By 1977, the railroad no longer existed having completely merged with the Union Pacific Railroad. The building was sold and converted to condominiums for downtown residents.

> ➢ **Continue on 13th St. and cross Olive St.**
> ➢ **Pause after crossing for Stop 24.**

Stop 24:
St. Louis Public Library – Central Branch
(1301 Olive St.)

The Central Library building for St. Louis is one of the architectural treasures of the city. Cass Gilbert, who was the architect for the St. Louis Art Museum and the U.S. Supreme Court Building, designed this Italian Renaissance style building. The library opened in 1912.

Philanthropist Andrew Carnegie provided much of the money needed for its construction. He offered the city $1 million for the construction of the library. The residents of St. Louis provided the rest of the funds to complete the building and to purchase the books that are stored inside.

Inside the library are beautiful stained glass windows, hand-stenciled ceilings, and glass floors. This library is consistently ranked as one of the most beautiful libraries in the United States.

➤ **Continue on 13th St. to Stop 25.**

Stop 25:
Christ Church Cathedral
(1210 Locust St.)

The parish of Christ Church dates back to before the city of St. Louis was even chartered. In 1819, twenty-six congregants met in a building that was a former dance hall, to organize the church. This was the first Episcopal-Anglican congregation west of the Mississippi River.

The church building you see today began construction in 1859. The first service to be held in the church was on Christmas Day, 1867. The large tower and doorway was finished in 1911. The Cathedral is a great example of the 14th-century Early English Gothic style and is renowned for its stained-glass windows and Skinner organ. You need to go inside to see the real glory of this church.

Behind the alter is a sculpted wall, or reredos, that rises 35 feet high. The sculpted wall contains over fifty religious and biblical scenes. The reredos was carved in 1911 from stone excavated from the Beer Quarry in England.

The bells in the Cathedral tower came from the same foundry that cast the bells for the German Pavilion at the 1904 St. Louis World's Fair. The 5,732 pound central bell is the largest in the state of Missouri.

> ➢ **Continue on 13ᵗʰ St.**
> ➢ **Left on Locust St.**
> ➢ **Continue on Locust St. to Stop 26.**

Stop 26:
Campbell House
(1508 Locust St.)

The fur trading business in St. Louis in the mid-1850's provided a great deal of wealth for the city and many of its residents. In 1854, Robert Campbell, one of the leading fur traders in the state of Missouri, built this house for his family. The three-story townhouse was built in what was to become Lucas Place, the first truly wealthy neighborhood in St. Louis.

In 1938, the final Campbell resident of the home passed away and the house was donated to the city to operate as a museum. Because the home remained in the same family for close to 100 years, 90 percent of the furnishing inside are original. This provides a unique showcase of Victorian-style furniture, portraits, and textiles. The home is open for tours throughout the week.

- ➢ **Continue on Locust St.**
- ➢ **Right on 16th St.**
- ➢ **Right on St. Charles St.**
- ➢ **Left on 15th St.**
- ➢ **Left on Washington Ave.**
- ➢ **Right on 16th St. to Stop 27.**

Stop 27:
City Museum
(701 N. 15th St.)

Word's cannot easily describe St. Louis's City Museum. You really have to go inside to see this unique playground for the young and old alike. As you walk by the entrance to the museum, you get a general idea that this is one of the most eclectic and unique museums in the U.S. Notice the large praying-mantis sculpture overlooking the street, the Ferris wheel on top of the building, the school bus where kids and adults are climbing around on that hangs precariously over the courtyard. This is just a sample of what you can find inside.

The museum is housed in the former International Shoe Factory building. Artist and sculptor Bob Cassilly purchased the building in 1995 so that he could create a new kind of tourist attraction in the city. His idea was to create a huge, whimsical funhouse for the young, and young-at-heart. Using reclaimed objects found throughout the St. Louis metropolitan area, Cassilly designed the museum as a place to explore, showcase the history of the city, and just about anything else he could imagine. To honor the origins of the building as a shoe factory, the original antique braiding machines from the factory have been restored and customers can order colorful shoelaces while visiting the museum.

Inside you can explore the various floors and see such things as a circus museum, complete with daily performances. There are old cranes, old bridges, a human-sized hamster wheel, opera posters, insects (dead and alive), and a room showcasing native Missouri fish. Want to see Elvis, dressed as an alien, and sleeping in a coffin? Then you've come to the right place! And not to mention the dozens of tunnels and slides to take you anywhere you want to go throughout the building. There are tunnels underneath the building; tunnels you slide through, walk through, and crawl through. There's even a gigantic indoor treehouse you can explore.

This is not your grandmothers' stuffy old art museum. It's a must-see attraction while visiting St. Louis.

> ➢ **Continue on 16th St.**
> ➢ **Right on Delmar Blvd.**
> ➢ **Right on 14th St.**
> ➢ **Left on Washington St.**
> ➢ **Cross Tucker Blvd. and turn Right.**
> ➢ **Continue on Tucker Blvd.**
> ➢ **Left on Olive St. to Stop 28.**

Stop 28:
St. Louis Post Dispatch Building
(1139 Olive St.)

The St. Louis Post Dispatch Building was constructed in 1916. It was the first building in St. Louis that was designed in what is called the International Style. The limestone and granite structure was the original home of the leading newspaper in town – The St. Louis Post Dispatch.

In 1965, the façade of the building was completely covered over to give it a more "modern" look. The now "modern" building had all the charm of a concrete block. Thankfully, it was totally renovated several years ago. Layers of ugly concrete were removed to expose the elegant façade of the building you see before you today.

The offices and printing facilities for the Post-Dispatch moved to a new location several blocks away. Today the building is being converted into exclusive office spaces.

> ➤ **Continue on Olive St. to Stop 29.**

Stop 29:
Bell Telephone Building
(920 Olive St.)

This ornate, red sandstone and brick building was completed in 1889 for the Southwestern Bell Telephone Company. The seven-story building is designed in the Romanesque style. When the Bell Telephone company moved to larger office spaces in the mid-1900's, the S.G. Adams Company, a leading office supply company in St. Louis, operated out of the building for several decades.

From the mid-1980's until just recently, the building stood vacant. The building has been completely renovated into office and loft spaces. The first floor of the building is now a new grocery store called City Grocers. This is the first grocery store in downtown St. Louis in over twenty years.

> ➤ **Continue on Olive St.**
> ➤ **Left on 8th St. to Stop 30.**

Stop 30:
U.S. Customhouse and Post Office
(8th and Olive Sts.)

This ornate Federal Building in downtown St. Louis was constructed between 1873 and 1884. Architect Alfred Mullet designed the building in the French Second Empire style. Mullet also designed the Old Executive Office Building in Washington, DC.

The U.S. Court of Appeals for the Eighth Circuit met here from 1891-1935. The U.S. Circuit Court for the Eastern District of Missouri met in this building until 1912. And, the U.S. District Court for Missouri conducted trials here until 1935.

From 1935 until 1975, the building housed the main Post Office for St. Louis. For over three decades, the building stood vacant when the U.S. Post Office moved to a new location. In 2004, the building was transferred to the State of Missouri. The State completely renovated the building back to its former glory. Today, the building houses the downtown campus for Webster University and the Missouri Court of Appeals.

> ➤ **Continue on 8th St. to Stop 31.**

Stop 31:
Orpheum Theater
(416 N. 9th St.)

This Beaux-Arts style theater was built in 1917. The Orpheum Theater was financed by a local self-made millionaire by the name of Louis A. Cella. The $500,000 theater was initially used as a location for vaudeville shows in the St. Louis area.

By the 1930's, vaudeville was in a steep decline due to the new "talking picture movies." Warner Brothers purchased the building in 1930, and it operated as a movie theater until closing in the mid-1960's.

The building stood empty until the 1980's when it was restored as the American Theater. It was later sold to two local brothers, businessmen Michael and Steve Roberts. They renamed the building the Roberts Orpheum Theater. In 2012, the theater was sold and eventually closed. Today, renovations are underway to restore the building back to its former glory.

> ➤ **Continue on 8th St.**
> ➤ **Right on Washington St. to Stop 32.**

Stop 32:
America's Center
(701 Convention Plaza)

The America's Center convention complex is located in the heart of downtown St. Louis. The venue opened in 1977 as the Cervantes Convention Center. There are 83 meeting rooms and 502,000 square feet of exhibition space inside the convention hall. Also inside is the Ferrara Theatre.

Major conventions are held in the center each year. Some of the largest events have included the St. Louis Boat and Sports Show, the Working Women's Survival Show, and the National Rifle Association Annual Meeting.

> ➤ **Continue on Washington St.**
> ➤ **Left on 7th St.**
> ➤ **Right on Convention Plaza to Stop 33.**

Stop 33:
Edward Jones Dome
(701 Convention Plaza)

This $280 million sports facility is home to the St. Louis Rams National Football League team. The Edward Jones Dome opened in November 1995 with a game between the St. Louis Rams and the Caroline Panthers. The dome was originally called the Trans World Dome, but when Trans World Airlines went out of business, Edward Jones purchased the naming rights for the dome.

The dome is connected to the America's Convention Center and allows for large conventions, expansive trade shows, and rock concerts to be held inside the climate-controlled building. Motocross races and monster truck rallies are also popular events held inside the dome.

The Dome is also the site of the biggest indoor gathering in United States history. On January 27, 1999, Pope John Paul II held mass in the stadium. Over 104,000 people attended the service.

> ➢ **Continue on Convention Plaza.**
> ➢ **Right on 6th St.**
> ➢ **Left on Lucas St.**
> ➢ **Left on Broadway to Stop 34.**

Stop 34:
Union Market
(711 N. Broadway)

Public markets were once a vital part of the lives of the residents of downtown St. Louis. This grand building was constructed in 1866 as one of the newest and most innovative markets in the nation. Customers who came to shop for food and other items were greeted with terrazzo marble floors, white enamel brickwork, and polished metal countertops. A central refrigeration plant provided cool temperatures in every stand to keep food fresh. Unfortunately, the Union Market was never a commercial success as customers began shifting their buying habits to private grocery stores and meat markets that were flourishing in the downtown area. After only a few decades of operation, Union Market was closed.

In 1990, Charles Drury, owner of the Drury Hotel chain, purchased the building and converted it into a 4-star rated hotel. His careful renovations maintained many of the elegant features of the original market and there is a careful blending of the past and present inside.

> ➢ **Continue on Broadway.**
> ➢ **Right on Convention Plaza.**
> ➢ **Cross under the interstate as the road changes to Morgan St.**
> ➢ **Pause here for stop 35.**

Stop 35:
Laclède's Landing
(Between Eads Bridge and Martin Luther King Bridge)

Laclède's Landing is a small urban historic district in the city of St. Louis. This area is part of the original settlement founded by Frenchman Pierre Laclede. The Landing is a multi-block collection of cobblestone streets and vintage brick and cast-iron warehouses. Many of the buildings date from 1850 through1900. Today, The Landing is home to many restaurants, bars, and shops.

In 1849, a blaze began on the steamboat *White Cloud* and, despite the efforts of the volunteer firemen, the flames could not be contained. Much of the riverfront area of St. Louis was destroyed in the fire. Tobacco, fur, and lumber stockpiles readily burned. The fire eventually burned itself out, but not before destroying 23 steamboats and 15-square blocks of the riverfront. Three men lost their lives in the fire. The more fire-resistant buildings you see today are the result of the re-building after the great St. Louis Fire.

> ➤ **Continue on Morgan St.**
> ➤ **Right on 2nd St.**
> ➤ **Left on Lucas St.**
> ➤ **Right on Rue Royale (1st St.) to Stop 36.**

Stop 36:
Eads Bridge
(St. Louis Riverfront)

The Eads Bridge is one of the most historic and important bridges ever to be built in the United States. When the bridge was completed in 1874, it was the longest arch bridge in the world. The bridge is 6,442 feet in length – slightly more than a mile across the Mississippi River. The bridge is also notable as being the first steel arch bridge ever constructed. For that reason, many residents of St. Louis were fearful that the bridge would never hold the weight of train cars and pedestrians. To prove to the population that the bridge was safe, Eads had the bridge "elephant tested." It was a popular belief at the time that elephants had instincts that would keep them from stepping onto unsafe structures. In 1874, a huge crowd gathered at the foot of the bridge as an elephant from a traveling circus lumbered across the bridge. Crowds cheered as the elephant safely arrived on the Illinois side of the bridge.

James Eads was a celebrated engineer who first came into prominence by creating a diving bell for the retrieval of goods from steamboat disasters. During the American Civil War, Eads was the designer for many of the ironclad warships used by the Union Navy.

The need for diving bells, Eads most important invention, played a critical role in the creation of the bridge. The Eads Bridge caissons are still some of the deepest ever sunk in any construction project. The depths were so great that the first major outbreaks of "caisson disease," also called "the bends," occurred during construction. Without the use of the diving bells, the numbers of deaths caused during construction would have been tremendous. As it was, fifteen workers died on the project.

It took seven years to complete the bridge at a cost of over $10 million. On July 4, 1874 the bridge was officially opened and a 14-mile long parade of residents wound through the streets of St. Louis and across the bridge. General William Tecumseh Sherman drove the final spike on the railroad tracks.

The bridge has stood the test of time and is still in use today. In 1871, the bridge was strengthen when a tornado crumpled the east side of the bridge. It was re-designed to make it tornado proof. The design worked, as the bridge was once again struck by a tornado in 1896 and the bridge suffered no damage. Electric railway service opened on the bridge that same year and continued its service until 1935. As car ownership grew in the early 1940's, the deck of the bridge was replaced with concrete so that thousands of cars could cross the bridge daily.

In 1991, the bridge was closed to automobile traffic when the deck supports had deteriorated to the point that they could no longer be safe. In 1993, the bridge was reopened when a new light rail train began crossing over into Illinois. In 2003, a major restoration project fixed the deck supports and the bridge was re-opened for automobiles to once again cross the bridge. Today, Eads Bridge continues to allow cars, light trains, bicycles, and pedestrians to cross the bridge. Occasionally the bridge is closed so that various festivals and other celebrations can be held on the bridge.

> **This concludes your self-guided walking tour of Downtown St. Louis.**

3

OTHER SITES TO VISIT IN THE REGION

Forest Park and the St. Louis Zoo.
One Government Dr. • St. Louis, MO

Forest Park is one of the largest public parks in the nation. The park is best known as the site of the 1904 Louisiana Purchase Exposition World's Fair and the 1904 Summer Olympics. Attractions at the park include the St. Louis Zoo, the St. Louis Art Museum, the Missouri History Museum, and the St. Louis Science Center.

First Missouri State Capital State Historic Site
200 S. Main St • St, Charles, MM

From 1821 to 1826, the state capital of Missouri was in St. Charles, MO. A visit to this state historic site allows you to see the fully restored legislative chambers, while a visit to the interpretive center offers exhibits on the early history of the state of Missouri.

Anheuser-Busch Brewery Tours
12th and Lynch Sts. • St. Louis, MO

Tours include the historic brew house, the Budweiser Clydesdale stable, the beechwood aging cellar, and the packaging plant. At the end of the tour, those over the age of 21 are welcome to test drive a freshly brewed beer of their choice.

Cathedral Basilica of Saint Louis
Lindell Blvd. at Newstead Ave. • St. Louis, MO

This basilica, home to the Archbishop of St. Louis, is one of the most beautiful cathedrals in the nation. Inside the massive stone building is the largest mosaic collection in the western hemisphere. Masses are held daily and tours are provided throughout the day.

Ulysses S. Grant National Historic Site (White Haven Home)
7400 Grant Rd • St. Louis, MO

For many years, Ulysses S. Grant lived in this home that belonged to the family of his wife, Julia. Tours of the home are given daily. Here you learn that the man who defeated the Confederacy had once lived on a farm where slaves were kept.

Grant's Farm
10501 Gravois Rd • St. Louis, MO

This Busch family estate was once owned by Ulysses S. Grant. Today, there are animal shows, petting zoos, and a train ride through a wildlife preserve.

Jefferson Barracks Historic Park and National Cemetery
533 Grant Rd • St. Louis, MO

Jefferson Barracks was once one of the largest military camps west of the Mississippi River. Robert E. Lee and Ulysses S. Grant both served on this military base. In 1866, a national cemetery was created on the grounds. Military personnel from the War of Independence through the present day are interred within the cemetery.

Route 66 Sidewalk Plaques
7200-7400 Manchester Rd • Maplewood, MO

Maplewood, MO pays tribute to iconic Route 66. Walking the "Mother Road" along Manchester Rd. takes visitors down memory lane. Unique sidewalk plaques and murals enhance your walk.

The Magic House, St. Louis Children's Museum
516 S. Kirkwood Rd. • St. Louis, Mo

This nationally acclaimed children's museum offers hundreds of hands-on activities and fun, educational things for kids to do on a daily basis.

Six Flags St. Louis
I-44 Southwest of St. Louis • Eureka, MO

Looking for fun, excitement, and maybe a heart-stopping ride on some of the wildest rollercoasters in the nation, then Six Flags is just the place to visit. Hurricane Harbor, a 12-acre water park, is also included with the price of admission.

Ted Drewes Frozen Custard
Old Rte 66, 6726 Chippewa • St. Louis, MO

While much of old Route 66 is gone throughout the St. Louis area, one place has stayed the same. Ted Drewes has been a St. Louis tradition on Old Route 66 since 1929. Their frozen custard is so thick you can turn the cup upside down and not lose a drop.

Tower Grove Park
4256 Magnolia Ave • St. Louis, MO

This 289-acre National Historic Landmark park offers a quiet oasis in the middle of the city. Walking trails, birdwatching, and small festivals surround the Victorian-era pavilions. It's a great place to relax and unwind after a day of walking and sightseeing.

Cahokia Mounds State Historic Site
30 Ramey St. • Collinsville, IL

Just across the Missouri River, is the site of the largest prehistoric Indian city complexes and burial mounds north of Mexico. A visit to this site allows you to see the mounds up close. The visitor center offers exhibits on the original inhabitants of this region.

If you enjoyed this guidebook, we have many more to choose from. Got to www.wanderingwalksofwonder.com for more books and journals..

Walking Guide:
Hannibal, MO

Walking Guide:
Independence, MO

National Parks Journal

My Road Trip Journal

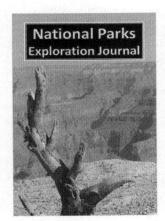

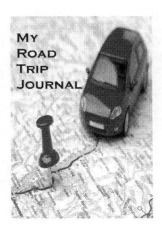

ABOUT THE AUTHOR

The author, Tom Alyea, is an avid walker, hiker and author of numerous books, guidebooks, and journals. He spends most of his time walking across the United States and around the world finding ways that he can rediscover a new life on the trail and motivate others to do the same.

Tom is also a member of the only national walking club in the U.S. – The American Volkssport Association.

Made in the USA
Las Vegas, NV
28 January 2022

42498373R00035